Analogies for Beginners

Written by: **Lynne Chatham**

Illustrations by: **Dean Crawford Jr.**

Prufrock Press Inc.
P.O. Box 8813
Waco, TX 76714-8813
Phone: (800) 998-2208
Fax: (800) 240-0333
http://www.prufrock.com

About This Book

An analogy is a comparison between two things. It points out the similarities or likenesses between things that might be different in all other respects. Analogies draw a parallel between the common characteristics of two things and cause us to think analytically about forms, usages, structures, and relationships. **Analogies for Beginners** introduces young students to both visual and verbal analogies.

In order to solve analogies, students need to analyze the elements of the puzzle, define a relationship between two things, and then apply this relationship to two other things. As students look for new relationships, creative combinations, or untried similarities, they will be exercising flexible as well as critical thinking.

Although the analogies in this book have been carefully thought out, young minds sometimes find relationships that are not as obvious but in their own right merit consideration. When students offer answers that differ from those on the answer page, discuss their answers and ask them to explain their line of reasoning. This strategy will encourage students to develop their reasoning abilities more than just seeking the one correct answer, and in the long run, this is the most valuable lesson.

Contents

Look at the first two figures. Decide how they are related. Find the figure that is related to the third figure in the same way that the first two figures are related. Draw a circle around the figure that completes the analogy.

Example: ○ is like ◯   as   ▫ is like ☐

1. ☆ is like ☆ as ◯ is like	a. ○ b. ● c. ⊕
2. ✳ is like ✳ as ⬡ is like	a. ⬡ b. ⬡ c. ⬡
3. ◎ is like ⊙ as ▯ is like	a. ▯ b. ▭ c. ▯
4. **A** is like A as **N** is like	a. n b. N c. z
5. ◻ is like ◻ as ⬡ is like	a. ⬡ b. ⬡ c. ⬡
6. △▽ is like △▽ as ○○ is like	a. ◎ b. ○○ c. ○ ○
7. △ is like △△ as ☐ is like	a. ▫☐ b. ☐▫ c. ▣

Look at the first two figures. Decide how they are related. Find the figure that is related to the third figure in the same way that the first two figures are related. Draw a circle around the figure that completes the analogy.

Example: ◯ is like ⊖   as   △ is like △̲

1. ⊠ is like ☐ as ⬡⊛ is like   a. ⬡   b. ⬡⊠   c. ⬡⟋

2. ◯ is like ⊙ as ◻ is like   a. ◸⊘   b. ◻▫   c. ◻◯

3. ⬡ is like ⬡̲ as ☐ is like   a. ◻△   b. ◻ c. ☐

4. ⊕ is like ◯ as ⊠ is like   a. ◻⟋   b. ⊞   c. ☐

5. ✳ is like ☆ as ✡ is like   a. △   b. ▽   c. ▼▼▼

6. ▽ is like ◺ as ◯ is like   a. ⊙   b. ◉   c. ☀

7. ⬛cube is like ☐ as △pyramid is like   a. ∇cone   b. △   c. △prism

Look at the first two figures. Decide how they are related. Find the figure that is related to the third figure in the same way that the first two figures are related. Draw a circle around the figure that completes the analogy.

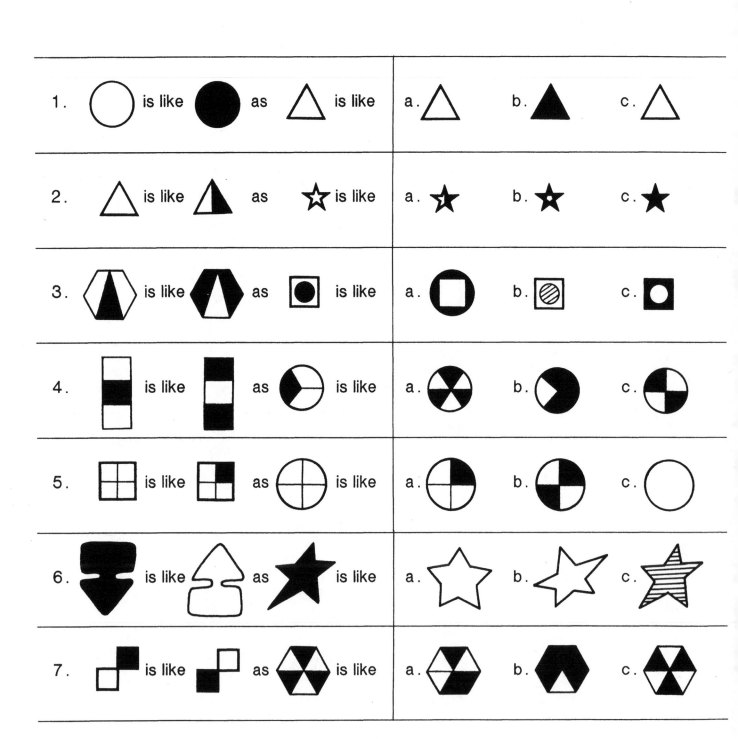

Look at the first two figures. Decide how they are related. Find the figure that is related to the third figure in the same way that the first two figures are related. Draw a circle around the figure that completes the analogy.

Example: ——➤ is like ◄—— as is like

---

1. **123** is like **321** as **abc** is like   a. **bca**   b. **ABC**   c. **cba**

---

2.   is like as is like   a.   b.   c.

---

3. is like as is like   a.   b.   c.

---

4. is like as is like   a.   b.   c.

---

5. is like as is like   a.   b.   c.

---

6. ₀○○ is like ○○₀ as △△△ is like   a.   b.   c.

---

7. is like as is like   a.   b.   c.

Look at the first two figures. Decide how they are related. Find the figure that is related to the third figure in the same way that the first two figures are related. Draw a circle around the figure that completes the analogy.

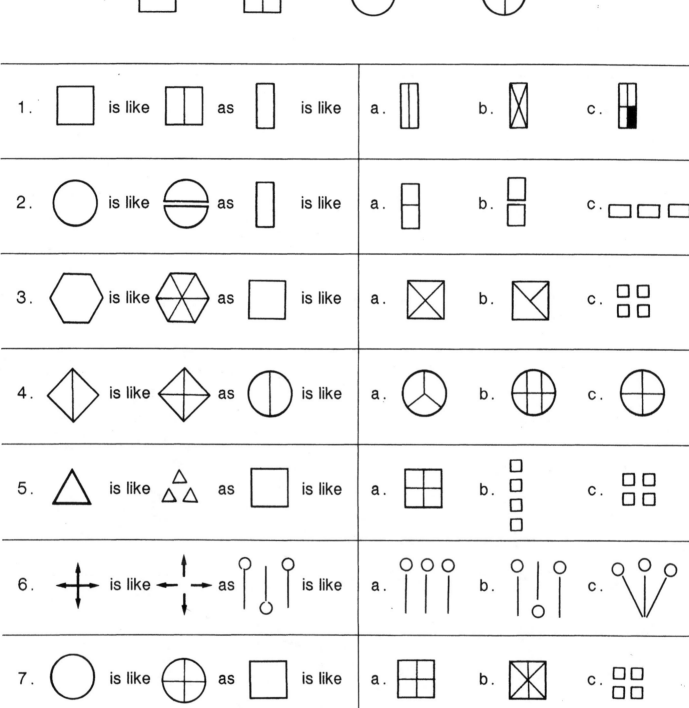

Look at the first two figures. Decide how they are related. Find the figure that is related to the third figure in the same way that the first two figures are related. Draw a circle around the figure that completes the analogy.

Example: L is like ⌐ as F is like Ⅱ

---

1. → is like ↑ as ▭ is like   a.   b. ▯   c.

---

2. **6** is like **9** as **p** is like   a. **q**   b. **d**   c. **b**

---

3. + is like ✕ as ☐ is like   a. ☐☐   b. ◇   c. ◇

---

4. △ is like ▽ as is like   a. A   b.   c. A

---

5. ●○○ is like ○○● as is like   a. ☐   b.   c. ☐

---

6. ♡ is like as is like   a.   b.   c.

---

7.   is like as  is like   a.    b.   c.

  © 2005 Prufrock Press Inc - Analogies for Beginners

Look at the first two figures. Decide how they are related. Find the figure that is related to the third figure in the same way that the first two figures are related. Draw a circle around the figure that completes the analogy.

Example: is like   as △ △ is like

---

1. ▢ is like ◉ as ▽ is like | a. ▽ | b. ▣ | c. △ ▢

---

2. ⬡ is like ⬡ as ▯ is like | a. | b. | c.

---

3. is like as o o o o is like | a. ○○○○ | b. ○○○○ | c. ○○○

---

4. O▢O is like ▢O▢ as −✪− is like | a. ✪−✪ | b. ✪✪✪ | c. ✪−✪−✪

---

5. is like ⬭⬭ as is like | a. ▭ | b. ▱ | c. ▭

---

6. ▢★ is like ▣ as ▽○ is like | a. ▼ | b. ▽ | c. △

---

7. △△△ is like △△△ as ○▢△ is like | a. ○△▢ | b. ▽▢○ | c. △▢○

10

Look at the first two figures. Decide how they are related. Find the figure that is related to the third figure in the same way that the first two figures are related. Draw a circle around the figure that completes the analogy.

Example: *addition* is like + as *equal* is like =

1. L   is like ⌐   as B   is like   a. ꓭ   b. ꓭ   c. **B**

2. 1 2 3   is like 4 5 6   as 4 5 6   is like   a. 1 2 3   b. 6 5 4   c. 7 8 9

3. +   is like —   as A   is like   a. ∧   b. Ɐ   c. V

4. ▭   is like ⊠   as △   is like   a. ▽   b. △   c. ◿

5. H   is like GHI   as M   is like   a. AMX   b. MNO   c. LMN

6. →   is like ⇶   as ◯   is like   a.   b.   c.

7. ☀   is like ◯   as 👁   is like   a.   b.   c.

Look at the first two figures. Decide how they are related. Find the figure that is related to the third figure in the same way that the first two figures are related. Draw a circle around the figure that completes the analogy.

Example: *fifty* is like **50** as *ninth* is like **9th**

1.   △ is like △ as □ is like   a. □   b. ▦   c. □□

2.   □ is like ◇ as △ is like   a. ◁△   b. ▷   c. △⦁

3.   ☼ is like ○ as 🦠 is like   a. ⬭⬭   b. ⬭⬭   c. ⬭

4.   △ is like □ as □ is like   a. ⬠   b. ⬡   c. ▧

5.   ▱ is like ▱ as ⬲ is like   a. ⊕   b. ⊖   c. ⬐

6.   **p** is like **q** as **b** is like   a. **d**   b. **p**   c. **σ**

7.   △ is like △ as → is like   a. ←   b. ↱   c. →

Look at the first two figures. Decide how they are related. Find the figure that is related to the third figure in the same way that the first two figures are related. Draw a circle around the figure that completes the analogy.

Example:  is like as is like

---

1. is like as is like   a.   b.   c.

---

2. is like as  is like   a.   b. ★   c.

---

3. **S** is like **$** as is like   a.   b.   c. □

---

4. **2** is like **3** as **M** is like   a. **M**   b. **N**   c. **N**

---

5. is like as is like   a.   b.   c.

---

6. is like  as is like   a.   b. ⬢   c. ⬣

---

7. **[** is like **Ǝ** as **V** is like   a. **A**   b. **Ɐ**   c. **>**

Look at the first two figures. Decide how they are related. Find the figure that is related to the third figure in the same way that the first two figures are related. Draw a circle around the figure that completes the analogy.

Example: ⊕ is like ⊕ as ◰ is like ◳

1.	**p** is like **d** as **L** is like	a. ⌐ b. ⌐ c. ⌐
2.	▭ is like ▯ as 🔲 is like	a. ⊡ b. ▯ c. ▢▢▢
3.	▨ is like ▨ as ◍ is like	a. ◍ b. ● c. ⊕
4.	♡ is like ♡ as ▢ is like	a. ◇ b. ■ c. 🎁
5.	▣ is like ⬚ as △ is like	a. △ b. ○△ c. △○
6.	⊞ is like ⊞ as ⊟ is like	a. ▢▢▢ b. ▤ c. ▢▢▢▢
7.	**F** is like **Ⅎ** as **D** is like	a. ⊂ b. **◖** c. **◗**

Look at the first two figures. Decide how they are related. Find the figure that is related to the third figure in the same way that the first two figures are related. Draw a circle around the figure that completes the analogy.

Example: ← is like → as ↑ is like ↓

1. ⊏ is like E as Γ is like   a. ⌐   b. ⊔   c. F

2. — is like – – as — — is like   a. ℓ ℓ   b. – – – –   c. | |

3. | | is like ⊞ as | is like   a. ⊣   b. +   c. —

4. ⋈ is like ⋈ as □ is like   a. □□   b. □   c. ■

5. 4 is like □ as 3 is like   a. △   b. ⊿   c. △△

6. ▧ is like ▨ as ◣ is like   a. ◬   b. ◭   c. ◿

7. ▭△ is like △ as ⬡ is like   a. ⬡(dots)   b. ⬡   c. ⬡

Look at the first two figures. Decide how they are related. Find the figure that is related to the third figure in the same way that the first two figures are related. Draw a circle around the figure that completes the analogy.

Example: ACE is like EGI as 135 is like 579

1. ◯ is like ● as ☐ is like   a. ☐   b. ▣   c. ■

2. ▷ is like ◁ as D is like   a.   b. ⊕   c. D

3. ◯ is like (circle with tabs) as △ is like   a. △ (nested)   b. ✡ (star of david)   c. ✡ (open star)

4. ☐ is like (die with dots) as △ is like   a. △ (with dots)   b. ☐ (die with dots)   c. △ (with dots)

5. ○ is like ◯ as ☐ is like   a. ☐☐   b. ☐ (nested)   c. ☐

6. E is like Ш as 8 is like   a. ∞   b. ⊖ (crossed 8)   c. ●●

7. ABC is like CBA as XYZ is like   a. XYYZ   b. ZYX   c. UVW

Look at the first two figures. Decide how they are related. Find the figure that is related to the third figure in the same way that the first two figures are related. Draw a circle around the figure that completes the analogy.

Example: ⋮⋮ is like ○○ / ○○ as ■■■ is like □□□

---

1. △ is like △/△△ as □ is like   a. □□/□/□   b. □□/□□   c. □

---

2. ▢ is like □ as △ is like   a. △   b. △   c. △

---

3. ●○● is like ○●○ as **ABA** is like   a. **ABC**   b. **BAB**   c. **CBC**

---

4. △(dots) is like ⋰ as ▣ is like   a. ▣   b.   c.

---

5. —— is like 〜 as △ is like   a.   b.   c.

---

6. ○ is like ● as □ is like   a. ■   b. □   c. ■

---

7. ⋮ is like   as ▲▲▲▲ is like   a. ▲/▲/▲/▲   b. ▲▲▲▲ / ▲▲▲▲   c. ▲▲▲ / ▲▲▲

Look at the first two groups of letters or numbers. Decide how they are related. Find the letters or numbers that are related to the third thing in the same way that the first two things are related. Draw a circle around the thing that completes the analogy.

Example
ABC is like DEF as 123 is like 456

1. 45	is like 46	as 78	is like	a. 79	b. 96	c. 98
2. star	is like tar	as late	is like	a. ate	b. eat	c. let
3. MNO	is like ONM	as PQR	is like	a. QRP	b. RQP	c. QPR
4. 4	is like 8	as 5	is like	a. 10	b. 19	c. 12
5. 45	is like 54	as 76	is like	a. 74	b. 77	c. 67
6. 9	is like 19	as 8	is like	a. 16	b. 18	c. 17
7. evil	is like live	as emit	is like	a. time	b. tiem	c. mite
8. cat	is like hat	as get	is like	a. let	b. got	c. lot
9. rat	is like tar	as 789	is like	a. 879	b. 978	c. 987
10. bar	is like bare	as dim	is like	a. dime	b. diem	c. 10¢

This page has analogies that are either similar (synonyms) or opposite (antonyms). Look at each problem. Decide if the first part of the analogy is showing two things that are similar or opposite. Find the word to complete the second part of the analogy. Write the word on the line.

Example
Synonym: large is to big as tiny is to small
Antonym: large is to small as tall is to short

1. up is to down as over is to _____
   under   above   there

2. yes is to no as empty is to _____
   half   none   full

3. big is to huge as close is to _____
   closet   far   near

4. stop is to go as give is to _____
   offer   take   gift

5. happy is to glad as hard is to _____
   solid   rock   soft

6. odor is to smell as funny is to _____
   silly   fun   clown

7. money is to cash as dog is to _____
   bark   cat   hound

8. happy is to sad as calm is to _____
   clam   excited   boring

9. flower is to blossom as trash is to _____
   dirty   garbage   crash

10. shrink is to grow as tight is to _____
    tights   close   loose

Some of the analogies on this page give a word and another word to describe the first word (a characteristic). Some of the analogies give a word and what it is made of (composition). Look at the first two words in the analogy. Decide how they are related. Choose a word to complete the second part of the analogy in the same way. Write the word on the line.

Example
Characteristic: **yellow** is to **daffodil** as **green** is to **pickle**
Composition: **peanut** is to **peanut butter** as **apple** is to **apple sauce**

1. **links** are to **chain** as **recipes** are to _____
   cookbook   food   delicious

2. **sour** is to **lemon** as **sweet** is to _____
   eat   candy   pickle

3. **banana** is to **yellow** as **wizard** is to _____
   fairy tales   magical   elf

4. **lemon** is to **lemonade** as **milk** is to _____
   drink   glass   cheese

5. **ounce** is to **pound** as **minute** is to _____
   hour   time   second

6. **cat** is to **furry** as **porcupine** is to _____
   animal   prickly   pie

7. **whisper** is to **quiet** as **shout** is to _____
   yell   voice   loud

8. **jack o'lantern** is to **pumpkin** as **bean bag** is to _____
   beans   toy   throw

9. **dark** is to **black** as **light** is to _____
   bulb   white   shining

10. **hard** is to **cement** as **round** is to _____
    circle   square   rosy

The following analogies compare a general group and a specific member or example from that group. Some of these are written with the general group first, and some have the general group named after the specific example. Find the word that best completes the analogy and write it on the line.

Example
General – Specific: cereal is to oat as fruit is to orange
Specific – General: snake is to reptile as ash is to tree

1. **Mississippi** is to **river** as **Mars** is to _____

                  hot   planet   solar system

2. **month** is to **April** as **day** is to _____

          Tuesday   time   birth

3. **dance** is to **ballet** as **game** is to _____

         score   play   baseball

4. **fruit** is to **banana** as **dog** is to _____

         bark   beagle   mammal

5. **oxygen** is to **gas** as **gold** is to _____

         metal   shiny   jewelry

6. **meal** is to **dinner** as **money** is to _____

         spend   dollar   wallet

7. **food** is to **bread** as **beverage** is to _____

         milk   drink   sandwich

8. **hello** is to **greeting** as **sadness** is to _____

         cry   feeling   happiness

9. **frog** is to **amphibian** as **fudge** is to _____

         candy   brown   cookies

10. **jewelry** is to **ring** as **aircraft** is to _____

         fly   jet   submarine

Some of the pairs of words in the following analogies are things that usually go together. Other analogies on this page are pairs of things and the actions that go with these things. Find the word that best completes the analogy and write it on the line.

Example
Paired Items: **salt** is to **pepper** as **bow** is to **arrow**
Actions: **bandit** is to **rob** as **author** is to **write**

1. **ball** is to **bat** as **chalk** is to _____
   white   chalkboard   write

2. **cork** is to **float** as **anchor** is to _____
   boar   heavy   sink

3. **dog** is to **bark** as **sheep** is to _____
   Bo Peep   animal   bleat

4. **peanut butter** is to **jelly** as **cup** is to _____
   saucer   glass   drink

5. **pen** is to **paper** as **brush** is to _____
   hair   comb   bristle

6. **gym** is to **play** as **library** is to _____
   read   books   room

7. **bat** is to **hit** as **ball** is to _____
   round   frisbee   throw

8. **lock** is to **key** as **violin** is to _____
   instrument   bow   music

9. **needle** is to **thread** as **ham** is to _____
   eat   pork   eggs

10. **ladder** is to **climb** as **horn** is to _____
    instrument   bugle   blow

Some of the analogies on this page compare things that are parts of a whole. Some of the analogies name members of the same group. Look carefully at the first two words. Choose a word that completes the second part of the analogy in the same way. Write the word on the line.

Example
Members of the same group: chicken is to duck as snake is to lizard
Parts of the whole: tail is to cat as fin is to fish

1. nose is to face as toe is to _____
   foot   big   stub

2. core is to apple as cob is to _____
   corn   center   kernel

3. peppermint is to chocolate as Cheddar is to _____
   cheese   Swiss   yellow

4. jam is to jelly as pea is to _____
   green   vegetable   bean

5. cookie is to cake as coat is to _____
   shirt   warm   clothes

6. choir is to singers as team is to _____
   game   spirit   players

7. baseball is to basketball as glue is to _____
   sticky   staple   white

8. B is to alphabet as notes are to _____
   music   staff   black

9. guitar is to banjo as spring is to _____
   season   warm   summer

10. mane is to lion as tail is to _____
    last   head   monkey

© 2005 Prufrock Press Inc - Analogies for Beginners

Some of the analogies on this page make a comparison between things and where they are located. The other analogies compare things with their coverings or toppings. Look at the first two words in the analogy. Then choose the word that completes the second part of the analogy in the same way. Write the word on the line.

Example
Location: **letter** is to **envelope** as **story** is to **book**
Coverings: **hat** is to **head** as **shoe** is to **foot**

1. **fish** is to **water** as **bee** is to _____

   buzz   insect   hive

2. **film** is to **camera** as **money** is to _____

   wallet   dollar   spend

3. **clam** is to **shell** as **orange** is to _____

   fruit   juice   peel

4. **plant** is to **garden** as **animal** is to _____

   dog   farm   insect

5. **book** is to **library** as **clown** is to _____

   funny   make up   circus

6. **frosting** is to **cake** as **roof** is to _____

   house   top   slanted

7. **car** is to **garage** as **bed** is to _____

   sleep   bedroom   blanket

8. **blanket** is to **bed** as **carpet** is to _____

   rug   fuzzy   floor

9. **mask** is to **face** as **bracelet** is to _____

   jewelry   wrist   round

10. **boat** is to **water** as **airplane** is to _____

    air   fly   pilot

24

Some of the analogies on this page show things that are in some kind of an order (large to small, young to old). The other analogies show a comparison between things and their function or use. Look at the first two words and find a word that completes the second analogy in the same way. Write this word on the line.

Example
Degrees: good is to great as bad is to horrible
Function: oar is to row as ax is to chop

1. **brook** is to **river** as **hill** is to _____

        mountain   rounded   dirt

2. **bell** is to **ring** as **spoon** is to _____

        fork   stir   soup

3. **ear** is to **hear** as **nose** is to _____

        nostril   face   smell

4. **pink** is to **red** as **gray** is to _____

        color   gloomy   black

5. **jump** is to **rope** as **throw** is to _____

        ball   catch   game

6. **giggle** is to **laugh** as **stir** is to _____

        spoon   whip   batter

7. **shovel** is to **dig** as **broom** is to _____

        witch   sweep   handle

8. **bicycle** is to **ride** as **ruler** is to _____

        wood   inch   measure

9. **whisper** is to **shout** as **walk** is to _____

        run   legs   road

10. **child** is to **adult** as **lamb** is to _____

        chop   sheep   fluffy

This page includes many different kinds of analogies. Look carefully at the relationship between the first two words. Find the word that is related to the third word in the same way the first two words are related. Write that word on the line.

Example
dog is to **bark** as **bell** is to **chime**

1. **big** is to **little** as **last** is to _____
   first   face   back

2. **first** is to **second** as **third** is to _____
   fourth   three   next

3. **Lisa** is to **girl** as **maple** is to _____
   map   tree   birch

4. **finger** is to **hand** as **wheel** is to _____
   skateboard   roll   round

5. **white** is to **milk** as **red** is to _____
   pink   color   tomato

6. **add** is to **subtract** as **up** is to _____
   high   down   upper

7. **ring** is to **finger** as **hat** is to _____
   bat   baseball   head

8. **child** is to **children** as **school** is to _____
   schools   books   classes

9. **sweet** is to **sour** as **crooked** is to _____
   curved   road   straight

10. **tennis** is to **game** as **lark** is to _____
    bird   lovely   robin

This page includes many different kinds of analogies. Look carefully at the relationship between the first two words. Find the word that is related to the third word in the same way the first two words are related. Write that word on the line.

Example
glove is to hand as sock is to foot

1. car is to **wheel** as **wheel** is to _____
   spokes   round   bicycle

2. foot is to **leg** as **hand** is to _____
   fingers   mitten   arm

3. banana is to **peel** as **tree** is to _____
   oak   bark   wood

4. kitten is to **cat** as **puppy** is to _____
   duckling   cute   dog

5. plant is to **leaf** as **guitar** is to _____
   string   play   music

6. bee is to **buzz** as **frog** is to _____
   green   croak   turtle

7. fable is to **story** as **quiz** is to _____
   questions   test   school

8. lawn is to **mow** as **crop** is to _____
   harvest   corn   farm

9. vanilla is to **flavor** as **blimp** is to _____
   fat   flies   aircraft

10. half is to **two** as **quarter** is to _____
    money   four   three

This page includes many different kinds of analogies. Look carefully at the relationship between the first two words. Find the word that is related to the third word in the same way the first two words are related. Write that word on the line.

Example
ton is to **heavy** as ounce is to **light**

1. **butcher** is to **meat** as **baker** is to _____

   bread   bakery   mixer

2. **fabric** is to **thread** as **bread** is to _____

   soft   flour   jam

3. **first** is to **last** as **loud** is to _____

   children   noise   quiet

4. **toy** is to **plaything** as **luggage** is to _____

   baggage   pack   carry

5. **ABC** is to **read** as **123** is to _____

   numbers   456   count

6. **bottle** is to **jug** as **car** is to _____

   bus   drive   park

7. **hot** is to **fire** as **cold** is to _____

   coldest   ice   warm

8. **glass** is to **smooth** as **ant** is to _____

   insect   aunt   small

9. **New York** is to **state** as **Mexico** is to _____

   south   country   Canada

10. **pupil** is to **class** as **singer** is to _____

    song   chorus   voice

This page includes many different kinds of analogies. Look carefully at the relationship between the first two words. Find the word that is related to the third word in the same way the first two words are related. Write that word on the line.

Example
pencil is to eraser as cup is to handle

1. **dollar** is to **cents** as **book** is to _____
   pages   library   read

2. **child** is to **nursery** as **bird** is to _____
   fly   eagle   aviary

3. **nut** is to **shell** as **apple** is to _____
   peel   red   tree

4. **cap** is to **hat** as **milk** is to _____
   cow   white   water

5. **word** is to **sentence** as **letter** is to _____
   symbol   word   write

6. **button** is to **buttonhole** as **thread** is to _____
   string   needle   sew

7. **gallop** is to **horse** as **hop** is to _____
   frog   hippity   jump

8. **pine** is to **tree** as **brontosaur** is to _____
   large   old   dinosaur

9. **couple** is to **two** as **trio** is to _____
   tricycle   three   third

10. **sticky** is to **gum** as **cold** is to _____
    hot   illness   ice cream

This page includes many different kinds of analogies. Look carefully at the relationship between the first two words. Find the word that is related to the third word in the same way the first two words are related. Write that word on the line.

Example
rock is to hard as pillow is to soft

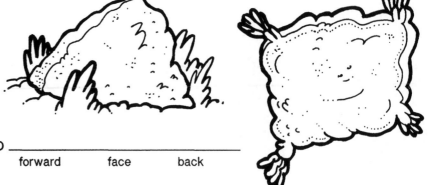

1. before is to after as front is to _____
   forward   face   back

2. knife is to sharp as ice is to _____
   water   slippery   winter

3. key is to piano as shoelace is to _____
   knot   bow   shoe

4. basketball is to court as baseball is to _____
   diamond   ball   player

5. feather is to bird as scales is to _____
   weight   fish   slippery

6. poodle is to collie as Chevrolet is to _____
   car   Chevy   Ford

7. motor is to car as heart is to _____
   body   beat   blood

8. hand is to wrist as foot is to _____
   walk   shoe   ankle

9. laugh is to funny as cry is to _____
   sad   tears   smile

10. instrument is to trumpet as mammal is to _____
    reptile   bear   furry

This page includes many different kinds of analogies. Look carefully at the relationship between the first two words. Find the word that is related to the third word in the same way the first two words are related. Write that word on the line.

Example
three is to **tricycle** as **two** is to bicycle

1. **feather** is to **pillow** as **air** is to _____
   plane   balloon   breathe

2. **top** is to **bottom** as **heavy** is to _____
   huge   hippo   light

3. **luck** is to **chance** as **alike** is to _____
   same   different   dislike

4. **teach** is to **learn** as **talk** is to _____
   speak   mouth   listen

5. **calendar** is to **days** as **clock** is to _____
   hands   hours   watch

6. **caterpillar** is to **butterfly** as **tadpole** is to _____
   frog   small   pond

7. **open** is to **close** as **beautiful** is to _____
   pretty   ugly   sight

8. **horseshoe** is to **hoof** as **arrowhead** is to _____
   arrow   sharp   stone

9. **elephant** is to **large** as **thunder** is to _____
   lightning   storm   loud

10. **insect** is to **ant** as **sport** is to _____
    player   fun   soccer

© 2005 Prufrock Press Inc - Analogies for Beginners

This page includes many different kinds of analogies. Look carefully at the relationship between the first two words. Find the word that is related to the third word in the same way the first two words are related. Write that word on the line.

Example
flower is to **lily** as **tree** is to **oak**

1. **dictionary** is to **book** as **dime** is to _____
   pennies   money   cents

2. **love** is to **hate** as **little** is to _____
   baby   large   small

3. **leg** is to **chair** as **spout** is to _____
   pour   shout   teapot

4. **ant** is to **anthill** as **astronaut** is to _____
   brave   spaceship   pilot

5. **lollipop** is to **stick** as **ice cream** is to _____
   cold   milk   cone

6. **heart** is to **blood** as **lung** is to _____
   breathe   oxygen   body

7. **pencil** is to **write** as **brush** is to _____
   paint   art   teeth

8. **bog** is to **wet** as **desert** is to _____
   sand   snake   dry

9. **butter** is to **milk** as **glacier** is to _____
   ice   cold   floating

10. **chapel** is to **cathedral** as **seedling** is to _____
    little   seed   tree

Answers

Lesson 1
1. a
2. c
3. a
4. b
5. b
6. c
7. a

Lesson 2
1. a
2. b
3. b
4. c
5. a
6. b
7. b

Lesson 3
1. b
2. a
3. c
4. b
5. a
6. b
7. c

Lesson 4
1. c
2. b
3. a
4. c
5. a
6. b
7. c

Lesson 5
1. a
2. b
3. a
4. c
5. c
6. b
7. a

Lesson 6
1. b
2. b
3. c
4. a
5. c
6. b
7. c

Lesson 7
1. a
2. b
3. c
4. a
5. c
6. b
7. c

Lesson 8
1. b
2. c
3. a
4. b
5. c
6. b
7. a

Lesson 9
1. a
2. b
3. c
4. a
5. c
6. a
7. c

Lesson 10
1. b
2. c
3. a
4. b
5. c
6. a
7. b

Lesson 11
1. b
2. c
3. a
4. c
5. b
6. a
7. b

Lesson 12
1. c
2. b
3. b
4. b
5. a
6. c
7. c

Lesson 13
1. c
2. c
3. b
4. a
5. c
6. a
7. b

Lesson 14
1. b
2. a
3. b
4. c
5. b
6. c
7. b

Lesson 15
1. 79
2. ate
3. RQP
4. 10
5. 67
6. 18
7. time
8. let
9. 987
10. dime

Lesson 16
1. under
2. full
3. near
4. take
5. solid
6. silly
7. hound
8. excited
9. garbage
10. loose

Lesson 17
1. cookbook
2. candy
3. magical
4. cheese
5. hour
6. prickly
7. loud
8. beans
9. white
10. circle

Lesson 18
1. planet
2. Tuesday
3. baseball
4. beagle
5. metal
6. dollar
7. milk
8. feeling
9. candy
10. jet

Lesson 19
1. chalkboard
2. sink
3. bleat
4. saucer
5. comb
6. read
7. throw
8. bow
9. eggs
10. blow

Lesson 20
1. foot
2. corn
3. Swiss
4. bean
5. shirt
6. players
7. staple
8. music
9. summer
10. monkey

Lesson 21
1. hive
2. wallet
3. peel
4. farm
5. circus
6. house
7. bedroom
8. floor
9. wrist
10. air

Lesson 22
1. mountain
2. stir
3. smell
4. black
5. ball
6. whip
7. sweep
8. measure
9. run
10. sheep

Lesson 23
1. first
2. fourth
3. tree
4. skateboard
5. tomato
6. down
7. head
8. schools
9. straight
10. bird

Lesson 24
1. spokes
2. arm
3. bark
4. dog
5. string
6. croak
7. test
8. harvest
9. aircraft
10. four

Lesson 25
1. bread
2. flour
3. quiet
4. baggage
5. count
6. bus
7. ice
8. small
9. country
10. chorus

Lesson 26
1. pages
2. aviary
3. peel
4. water
5. word
6. needle
7. frog
8. dinosaur
9. three
10. ice cream

Lesson 27
1. back
2. slippery
3. shoe
4. diamond
5. fish
6. Ford
7. body
8. ankle
9. sad
10. bear

Lesson 28
1. balloon
2. light
3. same
4. listen
5. hours
6. frog
7. ugly
8. arrow
9. loud
10. soccer

Lesson 29
1. money
2. large
3. teapot
4. spaceship
5. cone
6. oxygen
7. paint
8. dry
9. ice
10. tree

Common Core State Standards Alignment Sheet
Analogies for Beginners

All lessons in this book align to the following standards.

Grade Level	Common Core State Standards
Grade 1 Math	1.G.A Reason with shapes and their attributes.
Grade 2 Math	2.G.A Reason with shapes and their attributes.
Grade 3 Math	3.G.A Reason with shapes and their attributes.
Grade 1 ELA-Literacy	L.1.5 With guidance and support from adults, demonstrate understanding of word relationships and nuances in word meanings.
Grade 2 ELA-Literacy	L.2.5 Demonstrate understanding of word relationships and nuances in word meanings.